Violin Series

Third Edition

Violin Repertoire

6

Library and Archives Canada Cataloguing in Publication

Violin series [music] : repertoire album / the Royal Conservatory of Music.—3rd ed.

For violin with piano acc.
ISBN 1-55440-017-1 (v. 1).–ISBN 1-55440-018-X (v. 2).–
ISBN 1-55440-019-8 (v. 3).–ISBN 1-55440-020-1 (v. 4).–
ISBN 1-55440-021-X (v. 5).–ISBN 1-55440-022-8 (v. 6).–
ISBN 1-55440-023-6 (v. 7).–ISBN 1-55440-024-4 (v. 8)

1. Violin music—Teaching pieces. 2. Violin and piano music—Teaching pieces. I. Royal Conservatory of Music II. Title: Repertoire album.

MT275.V796 2006 787.2 C2005-905817-X

ISBN 978-1-55440-022-5

Violin Series
Third Edition

The present *Violin Series*, launched in 2006, is the third edition of this acclaimed series, originally published in 1992. It includes a body of essential repertoire and technique that has been carefully selected and edited to benefit students, teachers, and those who play the violin solely for their own enjoyment. This new edition has been further refined and expanded with the inclusion of an *Orchestral Excerpts* book, concerto movements in *Violin Repertoire*, Levels 5 through 8, and a wider selection of studies/etudes in each level of *Violin Technique*.

The primary goal of this series is to support the artistic and technical development of violinists as they learn their craft. Part of that craft involves a subtle understanding of the relationship between expression, style, and technique. The compilers' repertoire choices—which encompass a broad range of composers and styles—and tempo, bowing, and fingering suggestions have all been guided by the desire to present well-balanced volumes containing both traditional favorites and exciting new repertoire, edited with sound pedagogical principles.

Fingerings in particular must reflect a student's stage of technical development, hand size, and musical taste, and have been carefully chosen to develop shifting skills while maintaining established fingering principles. Any unnecessary repetition of fingerings has been avoided and every attempt has been made to conform to the technique covered at the corresponding level of The Royal Conservatory of Music curriculum.

This edition follows the policy that the bar line cancels accidentals. In accordance with current practice, cautionary accidentals are added only in cases of possible ambiguity.

For examination requirements of The Royal Conservatory of Music, please refer to the current *Violin Syllabus*.

Dr. Trish Sauerbrei
Editor-in-Chief

Contents

Concertino Grosso

I

Allemande

Milan Kymlicka
(b. 1936)

For examinations, play both movements.

1-55440-022-8 / 04

12
15
19
mp
f
22
mf
mf

26
mp
f
30
mf
34
a tempo
rall.
a tempo
rall.
f
mf
38
pizz.
rit.
arco
rit.
p

III

Sarabande
Andantino ♪ = 96 – 104
con sord.
mp
p legato
5
9
p
mp
mf
rit.
rit.
13
a tempo
a tempo
rit.
rit.

Concertino in G Major
op. 24
III

Oskar Rieding
(1840–1918)

22
mf
f
28
p
A
f
33
mf
ff rit.
rit.
f
37
a tempo
a tempo
f
mf

42
mf
mp
48
pizz.
count
53
arco
mf
f
p
mf
58
mf
f
mp
mf

63
mp
cresc.
p
cresc.
67
mp
p
71
mf
mp
f
mf
75
mf
mp
f
mf

79
mf
mp
f
84
ff rit.
a tempo
f
rit.
mf
89
94
ff

99
mf
f
105
111
ff du talon
8va
117
simile

Sonatina

II

Bohuslav Martinů
(1860–1959)

For examinations, play both movements.
Composed in 1937

20
24
28
33
A
f
p
mf

38
p
p
42
mf
46
mf
p
simile
50
f
mf
f
mf

III

14
mf
p
18
A
poco f
mf
22
ff
ff
f
27
f

32
37
41
46
mf
p
mf

51
mf
mf
mp
56
cresc.
cresc.
61
f
f
66
mf

71
77
84
88

92
97
mf
p
101
cresc.
cresc.
A
poco f
poco f
105
ff
ff
f

109
114
120
125

Sonata No. 5 in B flat Major

Thomas Augustine Arne
(1710–1778)
transc. Harold Craxton

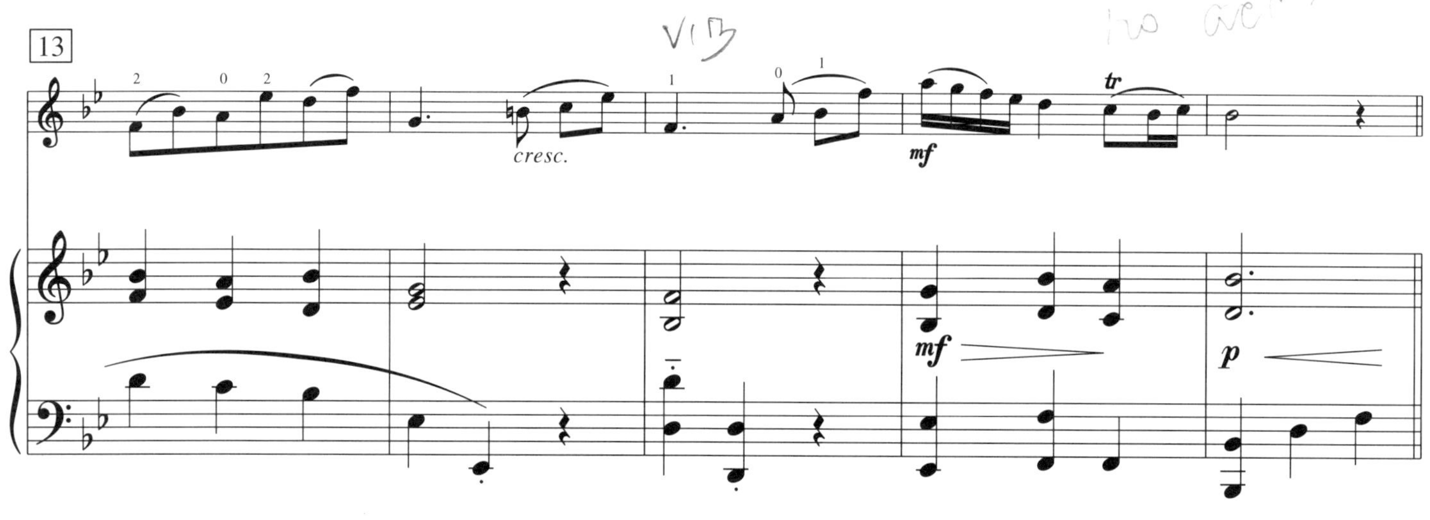

Source: *VIII Sonatas or Lessons* (London, 1756)

Quasi cadenza
dim.
cresc.

Gavotta

52
(b)
f
f
56
tr
(c)
p
p
59
p
cresc.
p
mf leggiero
p
62
cresc.
f
f
dim.
(b)
3
(c)
5

65
dim.
f
69
p
72
1 0
cresc.
0 1
tr
rit.
a tempo
76
tr
mf

80
tr
f
84
p
88
f
92
cresc.
allargando
ff

Invention in B flat Major

op. 10, no. 5

Francesco Antonio Bonporti
(1672–1749)
arr. Kathleen Wood

Source: *Invenzione da camera,* op. 10 (1712)

12
tr
3
15
tr
3
18
tr
21
tr
4
p
2
4
0
3
3
tr
poco rit.
p
poco rit.

Adoration

Felix Borowski
(1872–1956)

14
cresc.
f
cresc.
f

19
a tempo
rall.
p
a tempo
rall.
p

23
sul A
mf
p
mf
p

sul A
27
p
p
31
cresc.
G
cresc.
p
p
35
rall.
rall.
f
39
Allegro agitato ♩ = 92 – 100
f

43
mp
47
cresc. poco a poco
cresc. poco a poco
51
E
f
f
55
Tempo I
molto rall.
ff
fff
p cresc. poco a poco
molto rall.
ff
8va

60
f
f
65
p
p
70
ff
f
molto rall.
molto rall.
a tempo
a tempo
p
p
75
8va
A
A
E
rall.
rall.

Musette

op. 50, no. 3

César Cui
(1835–1918)

Source: *Kaleidoscope: 24 morceaux,* op. 50 (1893)

15
f
mf
20
poco rit.
poco rit.
25
a tempo
mf
a tempo
p
30
f
f

35
39
a tempo
rit.
mf
a tempo
rit.
p
43
48
p
poco rit.
pp
poco rit.
pp

Aucassin and Nicolette

Canzonetta medievale

Fritz Kreisler
(1875–1962)

In this style, *staccato* dots indicate slightly lifted bow strokes (brush strokes).
Source: *Four Pieces for Violin and Piano*

13
17
21
25
Poco più mosso ♩ = 80

30
cresc.
cresc.
35
41
p
p
46
D
Tempo I
p

51
56
61
cresc.
66
sfz
pp

Hornpipe

George Coutts
(1888–1962)

15
f
f
19
23
2nd time
poco allargando
Fine
f
mp
Fine
2nd time
poco allargando
f
sf
27
mp

31
35
39
43
mf
sf
f

48
mf
mp
53
57
mf
61
poco allargando
a tempo
D.S. 𝄋 al Fine

Romance

Max Reger
(1873–1916)

Composed *ca* 1902 in Munich

15
a tempo
p
f
a tempo
p
f
19
ff
molto espress.
rit.
a tempo
p espress.
a tempo
ff
rit.
p
23
cresc. molto
f
molto espress.
cresc. molto
f
27
p
sempre rit.
ppp
p
sempre rit.
ppp

Rustic Dance

Jean Coulthard
(1908–2000)

Source: *Little French Suite* in *The Encore Series for Violin and Piano,* book 6

17
naturale
mp
mp
p
21
attacca
f
f
f
24
sf
f
27
mf
mp

29
32
f
mf
sf
f
34
sf
37
ff rit. ad lib.
sf
sf rit. ad lib.

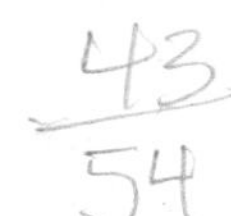

Souvenir de Sarasate

Fantasia espagnole

William H. Potstock

15
sf
f
rit.
mf
Meno mosso e tranquillo
19
mf
p
cresc.
f
p
cresc.
f
23
mf
f
rit.
più mosso
p
f
rit.
più mosso
27
sf
mf
f
mf
p
31
sf
f
f

35
dolente
p
mf
mf
p
mf
mf
39
f
mf
p rit.
f
sf
p rit.
43
f
p
f
p
mf
p
mf
p
47
f
mf
rall.
f
mf
rall.

51
dolente
p
sf
f
mf
55
f
mf
p
Tempo I
59
sf
mf
p
62
sf
f

65
p
sf
mf
68
mf
p
sf
71
sf
mf
f
ff
74
f

España

Ricky Hyslop
(1915–1998)

(a) the grace notes are optional 2nd time
Source: *String Knots*

17
Più mosso
mf
mp
21
25
29
p
pp

33
36
D.C. al Coda
D.C. al Coda
Coda
39
42
dim.
dim.

Jota

Timothy Baxter
(b. 1935)

Note: The jota is a fast Spanish dance.

15
p
p
p
con pedale
20
p
p
24
cresc.
cresc.
f
f
29
p
mp

34
mp
p
38
42
mp
47
pizz.
leggiero

52
arco
mf
mf
56
4
2
60
2
4
65
3
pizz.
mf
f